Hello, Family Members,

Learning to read is one of the most important accomplishments of early childhood. **Hello Reader!** books are designed to help children become skilled readers who like to read. Beginning readers learn to read by remembering frequently used words like "the," "is," and "and"; by using phonics skills to decode new words; and by interpreting picture and text clues. These books provide both the stories children enjoy and the structure they need to read fluently and independently. Here are suggestions for helping your child *before*, *during*, and *after* reading:

Before

- Look at the cover and pictures and have your child predict what the story is about.
- Read the story to your child.
- Encourage your child to chime in with familiar words and phrases.
- Echo read with your child by reading a line first and having your child read it after you do.

During

- Have your child think about a word he or she does not recognize right away. Provide hints such as "Let's see if we know the sounds" and "Have we read other words like this one?"
- Encourage your child to use phonics skills to sound out new words.
- Provide the word for your child when more assistance is needed so that he or she does not struggle and the experience of reading with you is a positive one.
- Encourage your child to have fun by reading with a lot of expression . . . like an actor!

After

- Have your child keep lists of interesting and favorite words.
- Encourage your child to read the books over and over again. Have him or her read to brothers, sisters, grandparents, and even teddy bears. Repeated readings develop confidence in young readers.
- Talk about the stories. Ask and answer questions. Share ideas about the funniest and most interesting characters and events in the stories.

I do hope that you and your child enjoy this book.

—Francie Alexander
　Reading Specialist,
　Scholastic's Learning Ventures

To my mother Lil Carrie, and my son Damon.
—G.J.

To my sisters Lorna and Terry with love.
—D.B.

ISBN: 0-439-20629-4

Text copyright © 2000 by Garnet Jackson.
Illustrations copyright © 2000 by Dan Brown.
All rights reserved. Published by Scholastic Inc.
SCHOLASTIC, HELLO READER, CARTWHEEL BOOKS and associated logos are trademarks and/or registered trademarks of Scholastic Inc.

Library of Congress Cataloging-in-Publication Data

Jackson, Garnet.
      Famous explorers / by Garnet Jackson ; illustrated by Dan Brown.
          p.   cm. — (Hello reader! Level 3)
      "Cartwheel books."
      Contents: Christopher Columbus — Jacques Cartier — Henry Hudson — Lewis & Clark.
      ISBN 0-439-20629-4
      1. Explorers — America — Biography — Juvenile literature.
2. America — Discovery and exploration — Juvenile literature.
[1. Explorers. 2. America — Discovery and exploration.] I. Brown, Dan, 1949- ill. II. Title. III. Series.
E101 .J325 2000
970.01 — dc21   00-029721

10   9   8   7   6   5   02   03   04

Printed in the U.S.A.   24
First printing, October 2000

Famous Explorers

by Garnet Jackson

Illustrated by Dan Brown

Hello Reader! — Level 3

SCHOLASTIC INC. Cartwheel ·B·O·O·K·S·®

New York   Toronto   London   Auckland   Sydney
Mexico City   New Delhi   Hong Kong

CHRISTOPHER COLUMBUS

As a small boy in Italy, Christopher Columbus lived near the Mediterranean Sea. He grew up walking along the shores. Sometimes he and his family sailed out on the water. Columbus promised himself that he would become a seaman when he grew up.

When Columbus became a man, he was ready to explore the sea. He wanted to find a shorter route to the Indies by traveling *west* through the Atlantic Ocean. The Indies were magnificent countries in Asia. Seamen went to the Indies for their riches and wonderful spices. But they had always traveled *east*, which was a very, very long way to go.

Christopher Columbus needed three ships for the voyage. He asked kings and queens from England, France, and Portugal for help. But the kings and queens refused to help him. Finally, he asked King Ferdinand and Queen Isabella of Spain. They said, "Yes."

In 1492, King Ferdinand and Queen Isabella gave Columbus three ships — the *Niña*, the *Pinta*, and the *Santa María*.

With 90 sailors aboard these ships, Columbus began his voyage. He was very brave, for no one had ever sailed this route before.

Columbus and his men sailed on and on. After about two months they saw land. "Look ahead, men — the Indies!" Columbus shouted, thinking he had indeed found a new route. "Soon we will have all the gold and silver and spices we will ever want!"

When Columbus and his men came ashore, native people greeted them. Columbus called these people "Indians" because he really thought he was in the Indies of Asia.

The natives were very friendly and giving. They believed in sharing.

They thought of the land just as they thought of the air and the water. They believed that it was a gift from God to all of His creatures — not something to be bought, sold, or claimed.

But Columbus claimed this part of the New World for Spain. He named the natives' land San Salvador.

Christopher Columbus went back to Spain and told everyone of the new world he had discovered. It was later called America.

Since those hundreds of years ago, many people from all over the world have come to this great land of the kind natives —and claimed much of it as their own.

JACQUES CARTIER

More than 500 years ago, there lived a great explorer named Jacques Cartier. He was the best explorer in all of France.

In 1534, the king of France, King Francis I, chose Jacques Cartier for an important expedition on the sea. King Francis wanted Cartier to find a northwest sea route to China.

The king had seen China's fine silks. He wanted some for the French people so they could have the finest of clothing. He also wanted Cartier to search for more islands and countries that had gold, silver, and other riches.

On April 20, 1534, Jacques Cartier began his first voyage. He was captain of two ships and 61 men. Early on, he reached an island that was full of different kinds of birds. It was called the Isle of Birds. He later found Brion Island, which was rich in berries and wild grains. Cartier also discovered an island named Anticosti, which had lovely fields and brooks. These islands were off the east and west coasts of Newfoundland.

However, Cartier's greatest discovery during this trip was finding the Gulf of St. Lawrence. He thought this body of water would lead him to Asia and to China. So he sailed on. But soon there were storms at sea. After sailing many miles, Cartier and his sailors returned to France. He would discover where the Gulf of St. Lawrence led on his next trip.

It was two years later that King Francis sent Cartier to sea again. On May 19, 1535, Cartier set sail with three ships and 110 men. He traveled up the Gulf of St. Lawrence and found the rest of the territory which is today Canada. With his crew, he went ashore to explore. On their trek, they came upon a tall, steep hill that Cartier called Mount Royal. The place where that hill was found is today called Montreal.

On May 23, 1541, Jacques Cartier went on yet a third voyage. This time he had five ships and 300 crewmen. They sailed to Canada and gathered what they thought was gold and silver. When they returned to France, the stones and crystals were tested. To Cartier's disappointment, it turned out that they were not real and were of no value.

Jacques Cartier never found riches or the northwest route to China. But because of his other exploring adventures, he helped many French seamen who came after him explore the mysteries of the sea.

HENRY HUDSON

Henry Hudson was an Englishman who came from a family of great explorers and seamen, his father and grandfather among them. On May 1, 1607, Hudson sailed off with his young son John and a crew of ten men aboard the small ship *Hopewell*.

They left England in search of a new and shorter route to Asia. The English people needed Asia's tasty spices to flavor their food. Asia had cloves, cinnamon, salt, and nutmeg. England did not have these spices.

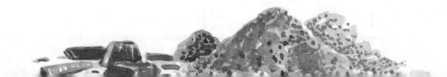

John wished to become a fine seaman one day. He watched his dad's every move as captain of the *Hopewell*.

Captain Hudson sailed on and on but he could not find the route to Asia. Finally, he and his crew sailed back to England. But he never gave up his dream.

On April 22, 1608, Hudson went to sea a second time hoping to reach Asia. Again, he failed. Then on April 16, 1609, he set off once more aboard the ship *Half Moon*. He had a crew of about 20 men with him.

This time they sailed into rough seas. Terrible storms rocked the ship, but Hudson sailed on. Hudson's search led him to a big river with the bluest of water. He and his men dropped anchor. This great river was later named the Hudson River after the explorer.

The land surrounding the Hudson River was called New Amsterdam. Today this area is New York State.

Henry Hudson and a crew of seamen began a fourth sea expedition on April 17, 1610. They suffered difficulties from icy waters, illness, and starvation.

Unfortunately, Hudson never found a route to Asia. But he is remembered in history for his other discoveries. He found a strait of water where no one had gone before. It is called the Hudson Strait. He also discovered a new body of water called the Hudson Bay. These waters were along the northeastern coast of Canada.

Many people since then have enjoyed the land and waters that Captain Henry Hudson found so many years ago.

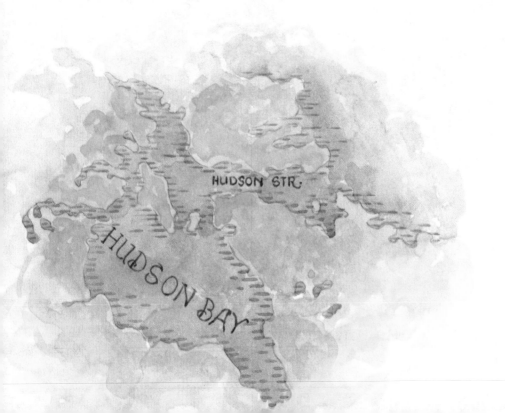

LEWIS & CLARK

Meriwether Lewis and William Clark were two boys who grew up more than 200 years ago in the 1700s. Clark came from a family of explorers. As a boy, he experienced many adventures with his father.

Lewis grew up liking books. He also liked to write letters. He was very smart.

When William Clark was 21 and Meriwether Lewis was 17, they joined the army. They became good friends. Lewis liked hearing Clark's stories about the adventures he had as a boy with his father. Sometimes Lewis would write these stories down in his notebook.

Since Lewis was so good in reading and writing, he was hired to work as President Thomas Jefferson's secretary when he got out of the army. He did an excellent job, and the President was very pleased with him.

One day, the President asked Lewis to head an exciting and important expedition. President Jefferson had bought some land from France. This land was Louisiana and all of the land between the Mississippi River and the Rocky Mountains. This was called the Louisiana Purchase.

President Jefferson wanted all of this land explored. He wanted the very best of reports about the findings. The President wanted to know about everything — from the rivers and mountains to the animals and plants. He also wanted the exploration team to find a route to the Pacific Coast.

Lewis suggested to the President that William Clark join him on this expedition. He explained that his good friend had come from a family of explorers and knew the ways of exploring. President Jefferson agreed, and that was the beginning of the team of Lewis and Clark.

Lewis and Clark began their trip in 1803. They started out on the Ohio River going toward the Mississippi River. Their first stop was the town of St. Louis, Missouri. In St. Louis, they got other men to join them on their adventure. When they left the town, they had a total of 40 men in their group.

Next they traveled up the Missouri River passing miles and miles of land. They saw many buffaloes and birds of all kinds. They met Native Americans who helped them along the way. A Native American woman named Sacagawea became their guide and interpreter. She knew all about the land and rivers. She was a member of the Shoshone tribe.

Sacagawea was very helpful to Lewis and Clark in many ways. Once one of their boats overturned and everyone panicked. Sacagawea came to their rescue. She saved many of the valuable supplies that had fallen into the river.

The scariest part of the journey was crossing the Rocky Mountains. These mountains had many narrow, curving trails. Sacagawea's people lived in the Rocky Mountains. She guided the explorers to her tribe.

When they met the Shoshone people, Sacagawea talked to them for Lewis and Clark. The Shoshone gave them horses and showed them how to get through the mountains.

Later Lewis and Clark met the Nez Perce Native Americans who led them to the Columbia River. This river took them to the end of their journey — the Pacific Coast.

During their adventure, Lewis and Clark studied forests, plains, hills, cliffs, and rivers. They studied animals such as Rocky Mountain sheep and grizzly bears.

The Lewis and Clark expedition lasted three years. They arrived back in St. Louis in September 1806. They were greeted by a crowd of people who celebrated their long journey. Lewis had kept reports and Clark had made maps. Thanks to these two men, many people were able to travel and settle throughout the new land.